Disaster!

Natural disasters of the world around us

Beatrice Adimola

Heinemann Educational Botswana (Publishers) Pty Ltd
PO Box 10103, Village Post Office, Gaborone, Botswana

Jhango Heinemann
PO Box 1259, Blantyre, Malawi

Heinemann Publishers (Pty) Limited
PO Box 781940, Sandton 2146, Johannesburg, South Africa

Heinemann Educational Books (Nigeria) Ltd
PMB 5205, Ibadan, Nigeria

Heinemann Educational Publishers
Halley Court, Jordan Hill, Oxford OX2 8EJ
A Division of Reed Educational & Professional Publishing Limited

© Beatrice Adimola 1999
First published by Heinemann Educational Publishers in 1999
All rights reserved.

Series Editor: Karen Morrison

Cover photograph from Digital Stock and Mark Henningsen (child)

Design by Jackie Hill @ 320 Design

Illustrations by Marjorie van Heerden, Maggie Brand and Kim Williams

Photographs courtesy of Panos Pictures / David Reed (page 28), Panos Pictures / Jeremy Hartley (page 8), Panos Pictures / Ron Giling (page 27), Rex Features (pages 6, 9 top and 21).

Printed and bound by CTP Book Printers (Pty) Ltd,
Caxton Street, Parow 7500, Cape Town.

ISBN 0 435 89893 0
99 00 01 02 7 6 5 4 3 2 1

Contents

About this book	4
Disasters make news!	5
What is a disaster?	6
Disasters in Africa	7
Floods	8
Drought	10
Storms	12
Lightning	13
Tropical cyclones	14
Earthquakes	16
Volcanoes	18
The mystery of Lake Nyos	20
Earthquake and volcano zones	22
Earthquake and volcano facts	24
Make your own volcano	25
Living disasters	26
Rinderpest	27
Plant invaders	28
Preparing for natural disasters	29
Taking action	30
Glossary	31
Index	32

About this book

In this book you will learn all about the disasters that affect our world. Read on, and find out more about:

- floods
- droughts
- cyclones
- storms
- earthquakes
- volcanoes
- pests
- diseases.

If you are not sure what a word means, look in the glossary on page 31.

About the author

Beatrice Adimola is Ugandan. She taught geography at Gayaza High School (a secondary school) for eleven years. She also helped to develop a new geography syllabus as a curriculum developer. She has travelled to different parts of the world including the USA, the UK, Israel, West and East Africa. She has visited many parts of Uganda as well. She enjoys taking photographs of landscapes, and reading and writing on the environment. She now works for the National Environment Management Authority as an Environmental Education Specialist and is involved with teachers and students in developing activities to conserve the environment. Some of the highlights of the students' work she has enjoyed are children's drama on the environment, pictures, poems, tree and flower planting, and improving the school grounds. She has co-written several books.

Disasters make news!

There are headlines like this in newspapers from all over the world. They report hundreds of different sorts of disasters every day. But what exactly is a disaster?

Nairobi floods leave thousands stranded

LANDSLIDE!

One million dead in Ethiopian famine

Locusts destroy crops in North Africa

Mount Pinatubo eruption devastates Philippines

Cyclone leaves 10 000 dead in Mozambique

Hurricane Mitch causes havoc

Early warning prevents flood disaster in India

What is a disaster?

When something causes damage to the environment and puts people in danger, we call it a disaster. When this event is caused by nature, we call it a natural disaster.

Changes in nature often cause disasters. A volcano erupts because of what is happening far below the surface of the earth. Other changes happen in the air because of the weather. When these weather changes are serious they can lead to disasters like cyclones or floods.

When changes happen in places where there are many people the effects are serious. A sandstorm in the middle of the desert is not a disaster. But if a sandstorm buries all the people living near an oasis it *is* a natural disaster.

People can also cause disasters. It is a mistake to build homes on land where landslides are likely to occur. Accidents, fires and war can all lead to disasters too.

Disasters in Africa

Most of the natural disasters which affect people in Africa are caused by the weather. Drought and floods destroy food supplies and cause large-scale famine. Fewer disasters are caused by earthquakes and volcanoes. Look at the map. What type of disaster is most likely to affect your country? What type is least likely to affect your country?

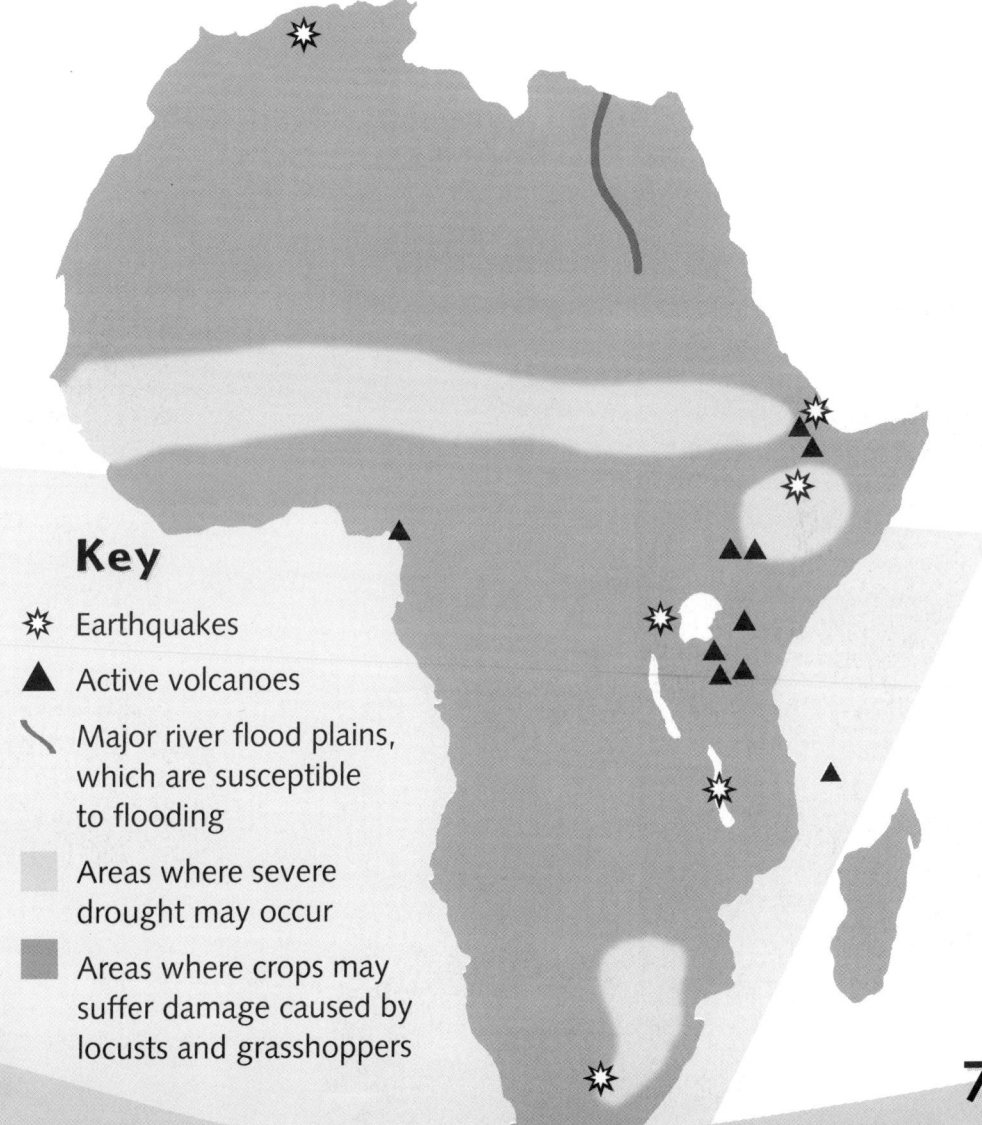

Key

☀ Earthquakes

▲ Active volcanoes

╲ Major river flood plains, which are susceptible to flooding

▢ Areas where severe drought may occur

▢ Areas where crops may suffer damage caused by locusts and grasshoppers

7

Floods

Floods happen when there is too much water in a usually dry area. Floods occur because of heavy rains, melting snow, unusually high tides and broken dams.

In 1988 heavy rains caused flooding in Khartoum in the Sudan. The effect of the floods was made much worse because people in Ethiopia had cut down the forests around Lake Tana. This caused a surge of water which flowed into the Sudan.

As a result of the floods:
- more than two million people were left homeless.
- almost half a million children were in the area. Some of them died from diseases carried by the water.
- valuable farmland was flooded and destroyed.

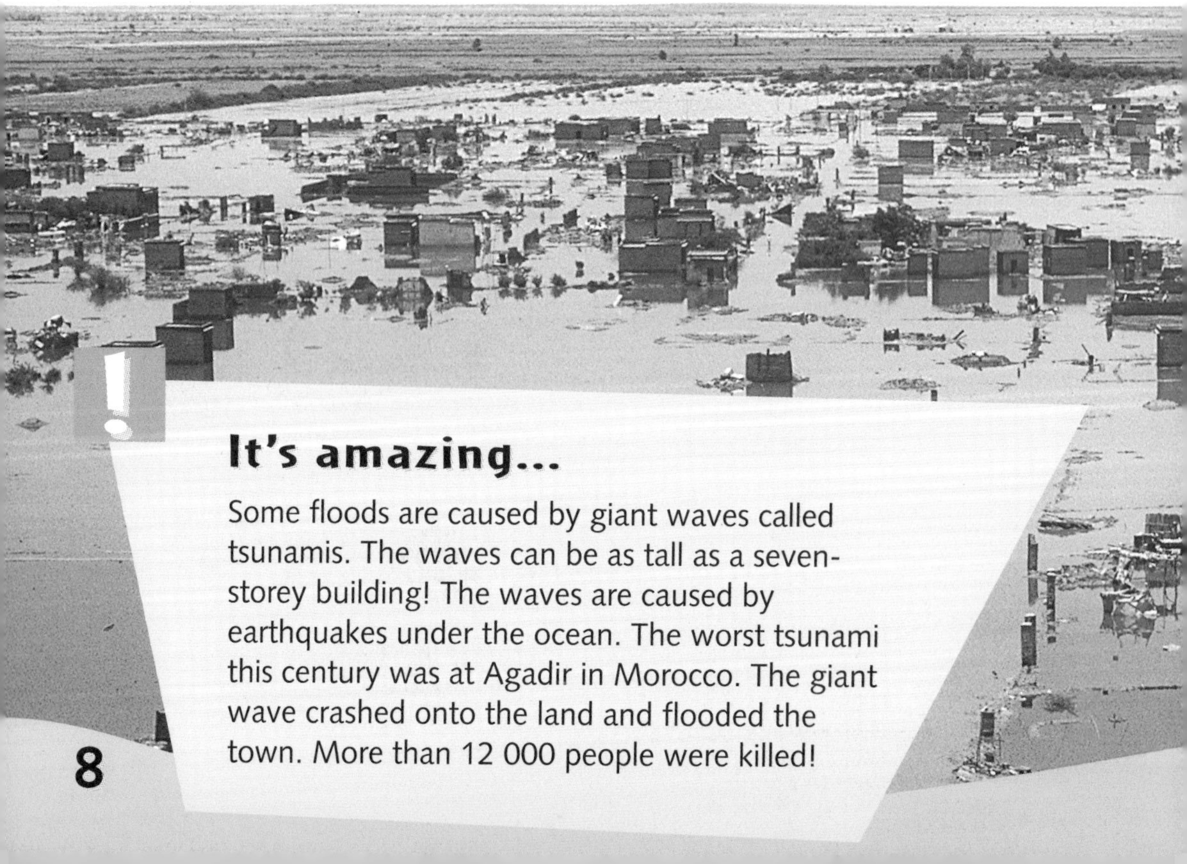

It's amazing...

Some floods are caused by giant waves called tsunamis. The waves can be as tall as a seven-storey building! The waves are caused by earthquakes under the ocean. The worst tsunami this century was at Agadir in Morocco. The giant wave crashed onto the land and flooded the town. More than 12 000 people were killed!

People can make floods worse by removing vegetation, cutting down trees, mining in in the wrong places and draining wetland areas.

Useful floods

Not all floods are disastrous. Farmers in many parts of Africa rely on yearly floods to make the soil fertile. During these floods the rivers overflow their banks and carry fertile silt onto the land. When the water drains away the silt remains behind on the fields.

During the floods in the Sudan 200 mm of rain fell each day. Usually, Khartoum gets about 250 mm of rain in a whole year!

Drought

A drought is a lack of rain or a shortage of water which lasts a long time.

Drought is the most common disaster in many parts of Africa. Drought leads to famine because crops and animals die from lack of water and food. People in farming areas are most affected by drought because they depend on their crops and animals to survive. In 1992 almost 18 million people faced starvation in southern Africa because of a very bad drought.

Drought will always happen because of changes in the climate. There is nothing we can do about it.

It's amazing...

Ethiopia experiences many droughts. It did not rain at all in one part of the country for three years!

Can we stop droughts?

People have different opinions about whether we can prevent droughts. However, experts do agree that people in high risk areas should be better prepared for drought. The more prepared they are, the less serious the effect of the drought will be.

We should all be careful not to waste water in good times as well as bad.

We cannot stop droughts, but we can plan better so they don't affect us as much. Here are some ideas for things we can do:

- Use local knowledge to watch for signs of drought
- Conserve the soil and replant trees
- Grow more food crops instead of cash crops
- Use dry lands carefully
- Store surplus food to last for one year
- Make a food policy so that there is always enough to eat

Storms

More than 1600 storms happen every day in different parts of the world! Big storms can cause damage to homes and crops. They can also lead to floods.

Most storms can be predicted. This means that people know they are coming and can prepare for them. Information and storm warnings are given on the radio and in the newspapers to prepare people. But storms can behave in unexpected ways. Some move faster than expected and others grow stronger and change direction. In these cases, many people are not prepared for a storm and the effects may be disastrous.

Not all buildings can survive a hurricane, when the wind speed is over 120 km/hr.

Lightning

Lightning is a flash of electricity from cloud to cloud or from cloud to ground. On the plateau in southern Africa lightning strikes every eight seconds! Lightning can kill people and animals but it is not normally disastrous and it is fairly easy to protect yourself. Look at the do's and don'ts on the list to see how you can be safe from lightning.

Lightning can cause more serious damage when it strikes trees and causes bush fires. In 1997 most of South East Asia was covered by a thick haze of smoke from forest fires, believed to be started by lightning. Fires which get out of control can lead to disasters.

Do

- Cut the branches off trees close to houses.
- Install a lightning rod.
- Stay indoors during thunderstorms.
- Lie down if you are caught outside. (Lightning will strike the highest point.)

Don't

- Plant trees too close to houses.
- Use the telephone during storms.
- Shelter under trees during storms.
- Stay outside during a storm.

I hope the man under the tree leaves me something in his will.

Tropical cyclones

A cyclone is a storm with very strong winds which move in a circular pattern. Cyclones are also called hurricanes or typhoons. Tropical cyclones are the most dangerous of all storms. They move at more than 70 km/hr and the strong winds can uproot trees, destroy buildings and overturn cars.

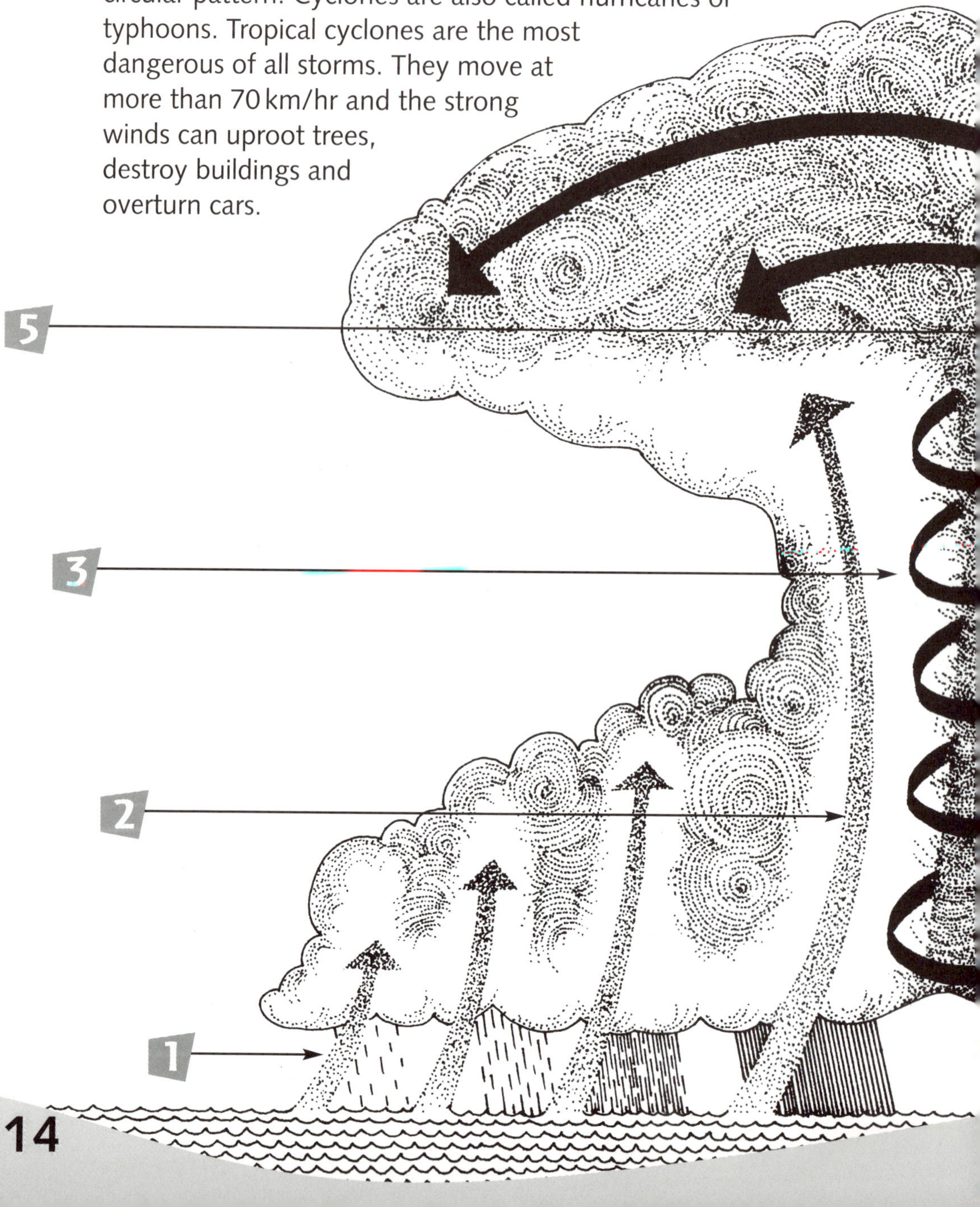

One of the worst cyclones to affect Africa was Cyclone Demoina. This storm hit the south-eastern part of the continent in 1984. It left 200 people dead and 10 000 people homeless. Farmers had their crops buried under the sand which the cyclone swept up.

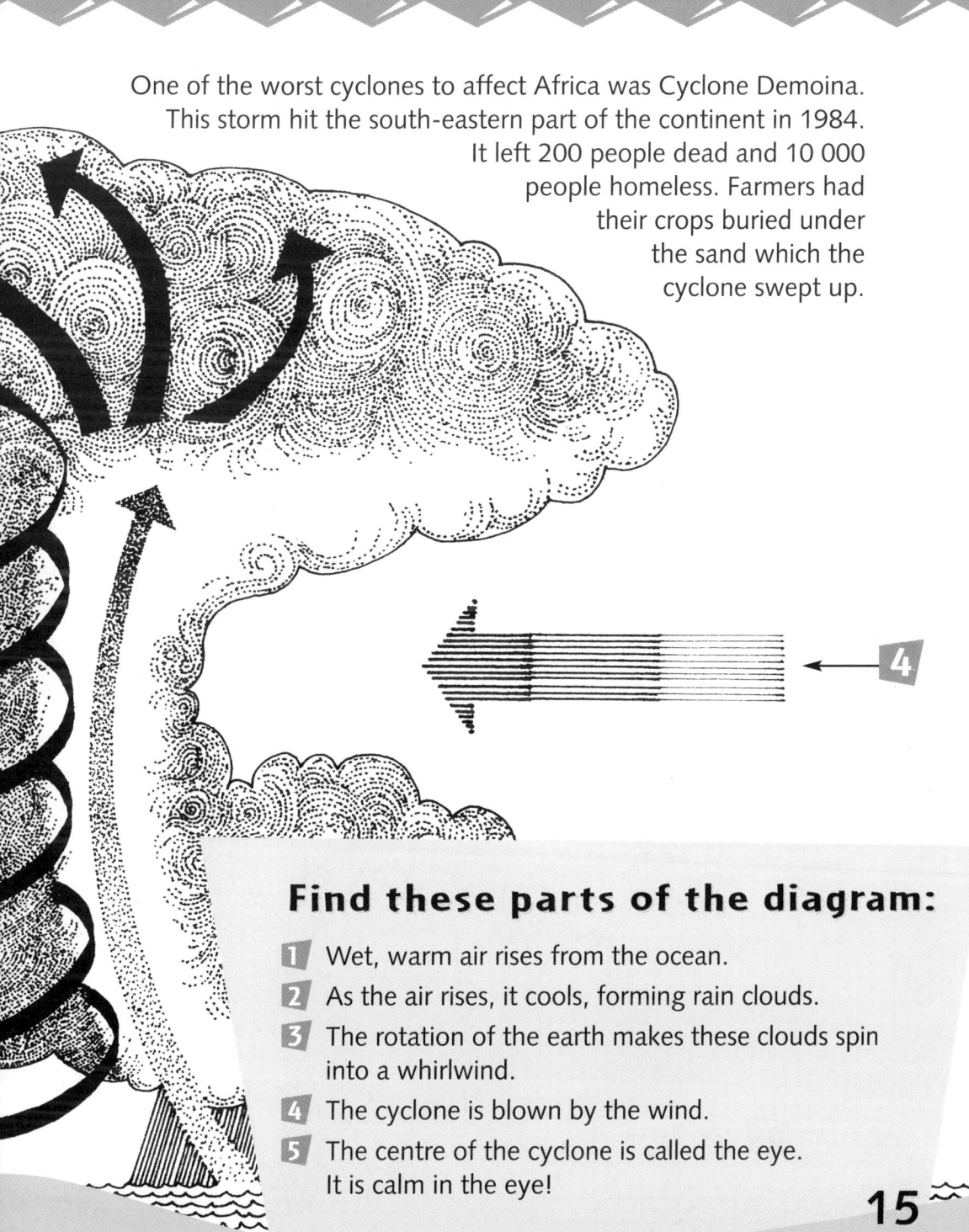

Find these parts of the diagram:

1. Wet, warm air rises from the ocean.
2. As the air rises, it cools, forming rain clouds.
3. The rotation of the earth makes these clouds spin into a whirlwind.
4. The cyclone is blown by the wind.
5. The centre of the cyclone is called the eye. It is calm in the eye!

Earthquakes

An earthquake is a strong movement in the earth's surface. Sometimes the movement is strong enough to rip open the ground. The earth's crust is made up of large plates of rock. When these rock plates move they bump against each other and cause shock waves which we can feel on the surface.

Human activity can also cause earthquakes. Near Lake Kariba in Zimbabwe people often feel tremors in the ground. These tremors are caused by the weight of the water in the dam.

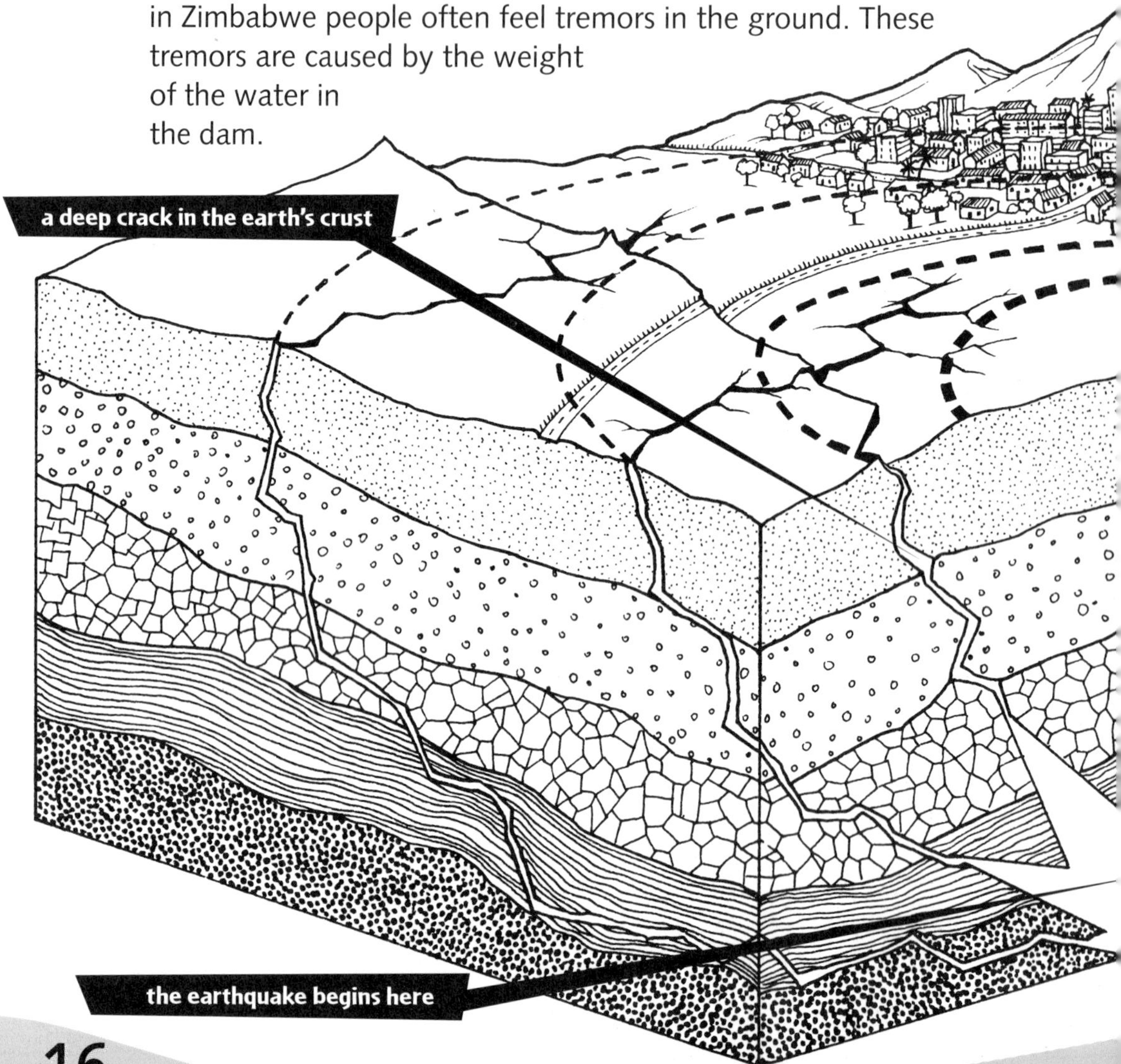

a deep crack in the earth's crust

the earthquake begins here

In mining areas people often feel tremors on the surface. These are caused by blasting (explosions) underground.

During a small earthquake the ground may shake, cracks may appear in walls and objects may fall off shelves. In a strong earthquake the ground shakes violently and cracks often open. Buildings and bridges are destroyed, roads and railways break up and fires start. There might be landslides on sloping ground. Sometimes whole cities are destroyed. You can see the results of the ten worst earthquakes on page 24.

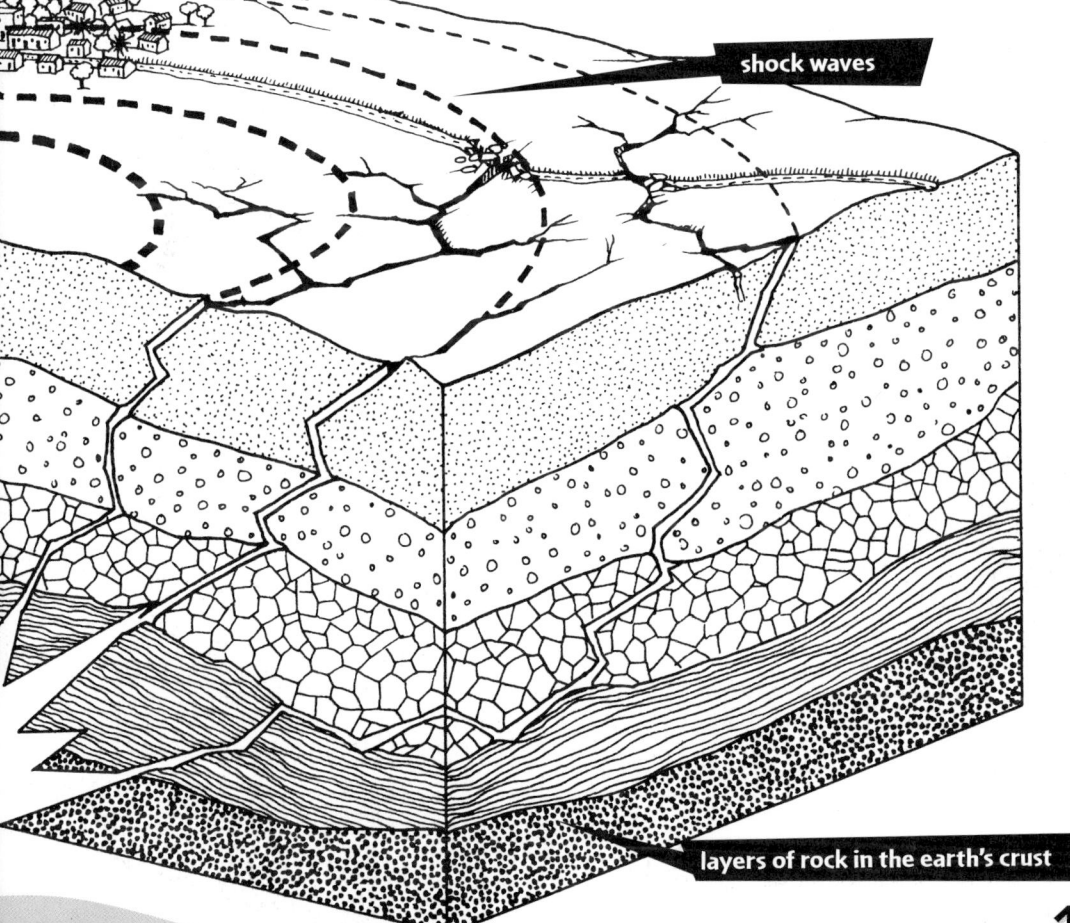

Volcanoes

When a volcano erupts, hot gases and melted rock shoot up from below the earth's crust. Melted rock which flows onto the earth's surface is called lava. When lava cools it turns back into rock. During an eruption, lava and volcanic ash can cover fields and bury houses.

Some eruptions are quiet. Lava simply rises up and flows from the opening of the volcano.

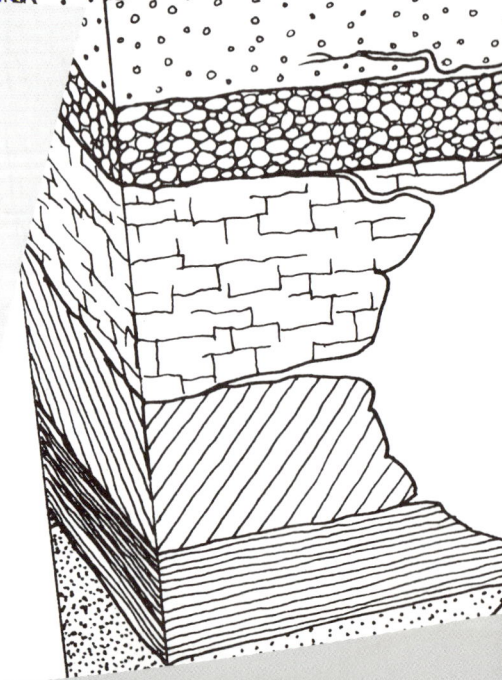

volcanic cone of layers of lava and ash

It's amazing...

People in Mexico watched a volcano grow before their eyes in 1943. A shepherd reported a small, smoking crack in the ground. Five days later the crack had changed into a 100 m high lava hill. The volcano grew higher and higher as more lava solidified on its sides. After ten days it was 200 m high! A year later it had grown to 500 m! This volcano is called Mount Paracutin.

18

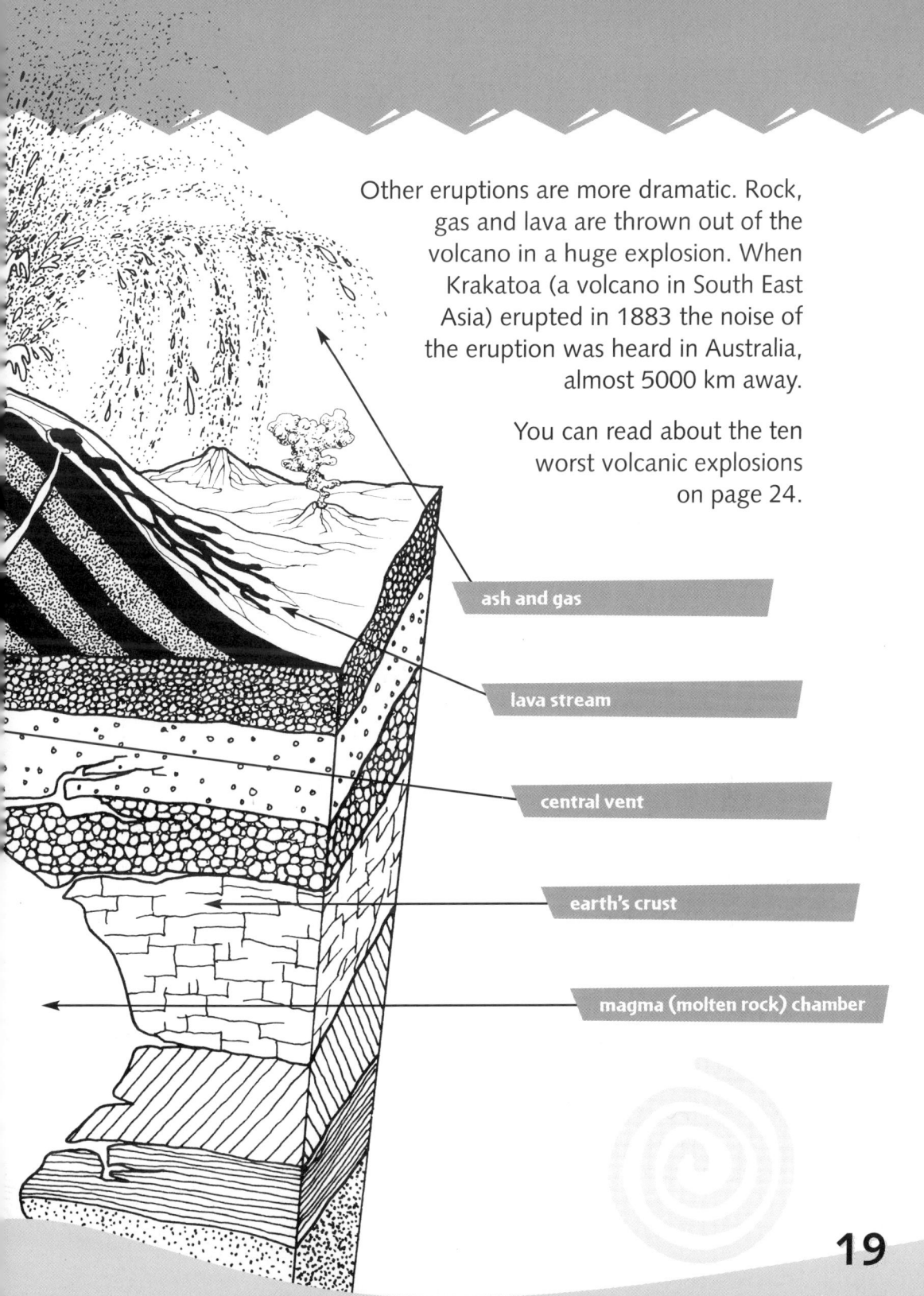

Other eruptions are more dramatic. Rock, gas and lava are thrown out of the volcano in a huge explosion. When Krakatoa (a volcano in South East Asia) erupted in 1883 the noise of the eruption was heard in Australia, almost 5000 km away.

You can read about the ten worst volcanic explosions on page 24.

ash and gas

lava stream

central vent

earth's crust

magma (molten rock) chamber

The mystery of Lake Nyos

One of the worst volcanic eruptions was invisible! It happened at Lake Nyos in Cameroon in August 1986 and killed 1700 people. There was no noise, no lava and no ash. What happened?

The volcano at Lake Nyos is under the lake. In 1986 the volcano erupted silently and produced a huge amount of suffocating gas. The gas bubbled up through the lake and formed a deadly cloud above the surface of the water. No one knew what was happening.

A slight breeze moved the invisible gas cloud to the edge of the lake and down into the valley where people lived with their cattle. As the gas cloud moved over the village of Nyos, people and animals collapsed and died from lack of air. The cloud then moved towards other villages in the area.

 ### Did you know...

Lake Nyos was not the only lake to produce this volcanic gas. In 1984 a similar cloud escaped from Lake Monoun (95 km south of Nyos). This cloud killed 37 people.

When news of the disaster got out, rescue teams from France and Israel rushed to Lake Nyos. They set up hospitals in the area and helped the people who had survived.

Scientists studied the lake and they continue to monitor the level of carbon dioxide gas in the water. They know they can't stop another gas cloud from forming, but they hope that they will be able to warn the villagers if it is going to happen again.

Lake Nyos disaster victims being rescued by helicopter.

Earthquake and volcano zones

Hawaii
Some islands are formed as a result of volcanic eruptions building up on the sea bed.

Los Angeles
People living in this city know they are in danger and take special precautions. Scientists monitor all movements to try and predict when an earthquake will happen.

Lake Nyos
A volcano erupted under the lake in 1986 killing 1700 people.

Mexico
Mount Paracutin grew to 500 m in a year.

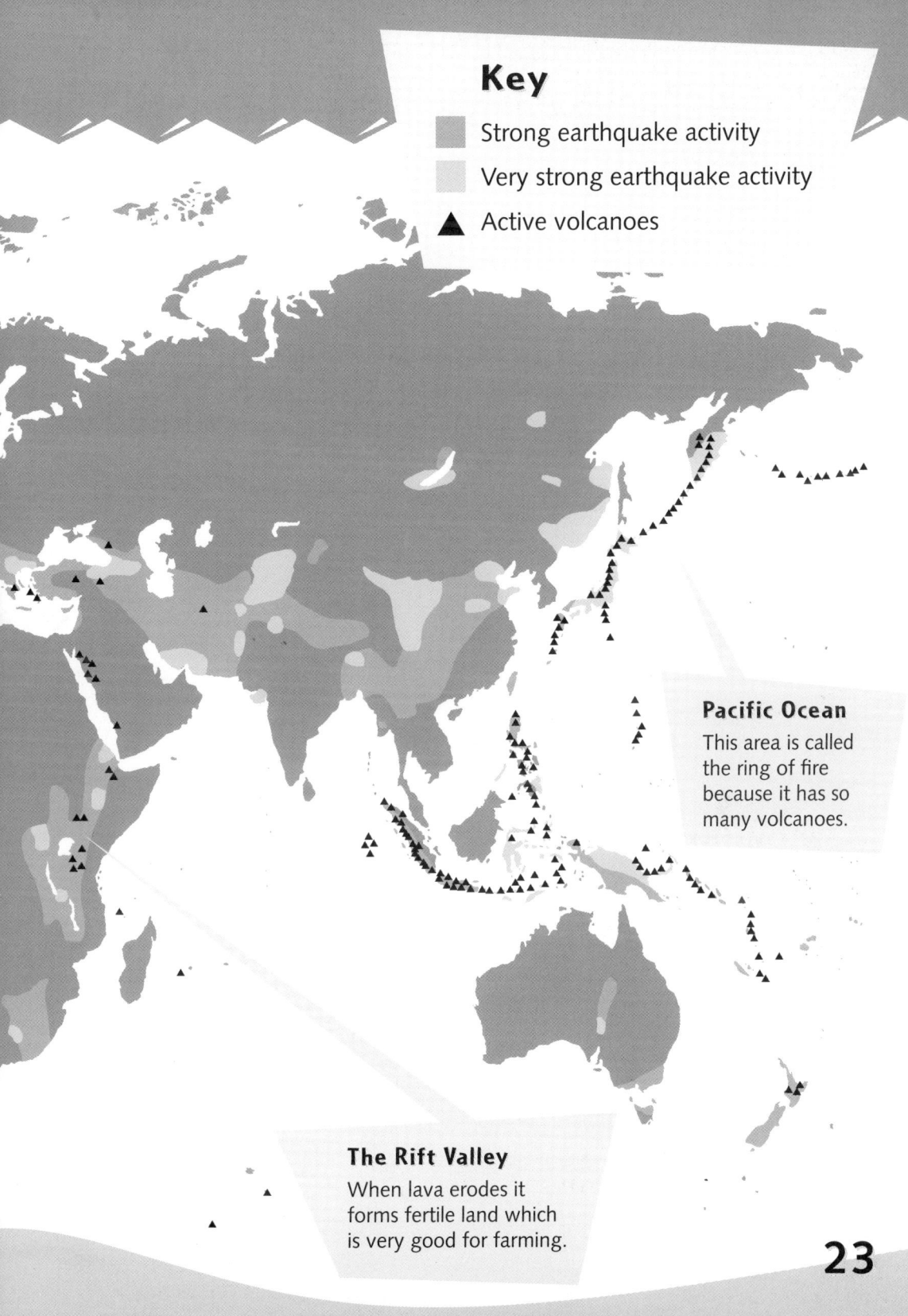

Earthquake and volcano facts

The ten earthquakes that have killed the most people

Date	Place	Number of people killed (estimate)
1976	China	242 419
1927	China	200 000
1920	China	180 000
1908	Italy	160 000
1923	Japan	142 807
1932	China	70 000
1970	Peru	66 800
1935	India (Pakistan)	50 – 60 000
1988	Armenia	55 000
1990	Iran	40 000

The ten worst volcanic eruptions

Date	Name of volcano	Number of people killed (estimate)
1902	Mt Pelée (Martinique)	40 000
1985	Nevado del Ruiz (South America)	23 000
1919	Keluit (Java)	5 110
1902	Santa Maria (South America)	4 500
1951	Mt Lamington (New Guinea)	2 942
1982	El Chichon (Mexico)	1 879
1986	Lake Nyos (Cameroon)	1 700
1902	La Soufrière (St Vincent)	1 565
1931	Merapi (Java)	1 369
1911	Taal (Philippines)	1 335

Make your own volcano

You will need:
- clay or a small bottle or jar and paper
- baking powder or bicarbonate of soda
- vinegar mixed with red food colouring or dye.

1 Make a model of a volcano using the clay or a bottle covered with paper. Use the picture to help you. If you are using clay to make your volcano, make a small well in the top (ready for step 2).

2 Put a teaspoon of baking powder (or bicarbonate of soda) into the opening in your volcano.

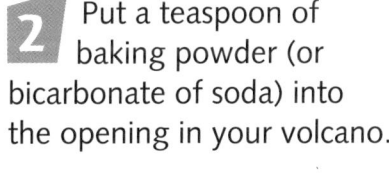

3 Pour in a little vinegar and watch it erupt!

Why does this happen?

Vinegar is an acid and bicarbonate of soda is an alkali (base). When they are mixed they react by fizzing and giving off gas (carbon dioxide). This reaction is similar to the reaction which causes bread or cakes to rise in the oven.

Living disasters

Insect pests, diseases and plant pests can destroy crops and animals at an alarming rate. If they are not controlled, they can cause severe famine and other disasters. For example, a very small part of a locust swarm can eat the same amount of food in one day as about 10 elephants, 25 camels or 2500 people!

Locusts move in large swarms. When they land, they eat crops and other plants and cause famine and starvation. North Africa is often affected by swarms of locusts. In 1993 a huge swarm appeared in the Sudan and moved eastwards eating every plant in sight. International agencies provided help to the countries facing invasion by locusts and helped to bring the swarm under control.

The Desert Control Organisation monitors the breeding and movement of locusts and warns any country which might be in the path of a swarm. These countries then spray their crops, which stops the locusts from eating them.

Devastation of food crops by locusts can cause famine.

Rinderpest

Rinderpest is an animal disease that spreads very easily. Infected animals die from the disease. In 1996 there was an outbreak amongst the wild animals in a game park in Kenya. The government of Tanzania was worried that the disease would cross the border and infect cattle. Their cattle had been disease-free for 14 years. International agencies like the Food and Agricultural Organisation (FAO) helped to set up large-scale observation and vaccination programmes. One million vaccinations were given in three months and the disease was brought under control.

Did you know...

The FAO works with governments to prevent and control disasters. These are just two of the diseases they have had to fight in the last few years:

- African Swine Fever: An outbreak in the Côte d'Ivoire killed 100 000 pigs. This was a disaster for local people as pork is their cheapest meat.

- Newcastle disease: This disease kills chickens. It affects the lives of small farmers who keep chickens for food and eggs.

Plant invaders

Waterweeds grow on all rivers and lakes in Africa. The water hyacinth looks beautiful but it takes the oxygen out of the water, and so fish die. It grows in a dense carpet that covers the surface of the water, and makes it difficult for boats to pass through.

At Zeekoevlei in South Africa, the water hyacinth got so bad that the authorities decided to drain the lake in order to kill the weed and improve the water quality. Once the lake was dry, local people who live near the lake pulled out the weeds. The winter rains filled the lake up again. It will take years to get rid of the weed completely as even one bit left behind will grow and spread very quickly.

Heavy machinery being used to clear waterweed.

Preparing for natural disasters

What can be done to prevent or lessen the effect of the main disasters you have read about in this book?

Type of disaster	Action that can help
Floods	◎ Building bridges and flood banks ◎ Removing mud from river beds so that more water can flow ◎ Replanting trees on slopes and in valleys
Drought	◎ Improved land and water management ◎ Growing suitable drought-resistant crops ◎ Farming with drought-resistant crops and animals ◎ Establishing early warning systems
Storms	◎ Warning and information systems ◎ Planting storm-resistant crops and trees ◎ Strengthening buildings and building shelters
Earthquakes and volcanic eruptions	◎ Establishing monitoring and warning systems ◎ Organising evacuation drills and regulations

Taking action

The Food and Agricultural Organisation (FAO) is one of the most important agencies in Africa. The FAO helps governments to prepare for and prevent disasters. This map shows you some of the work they have done in Africa in the 1990s.

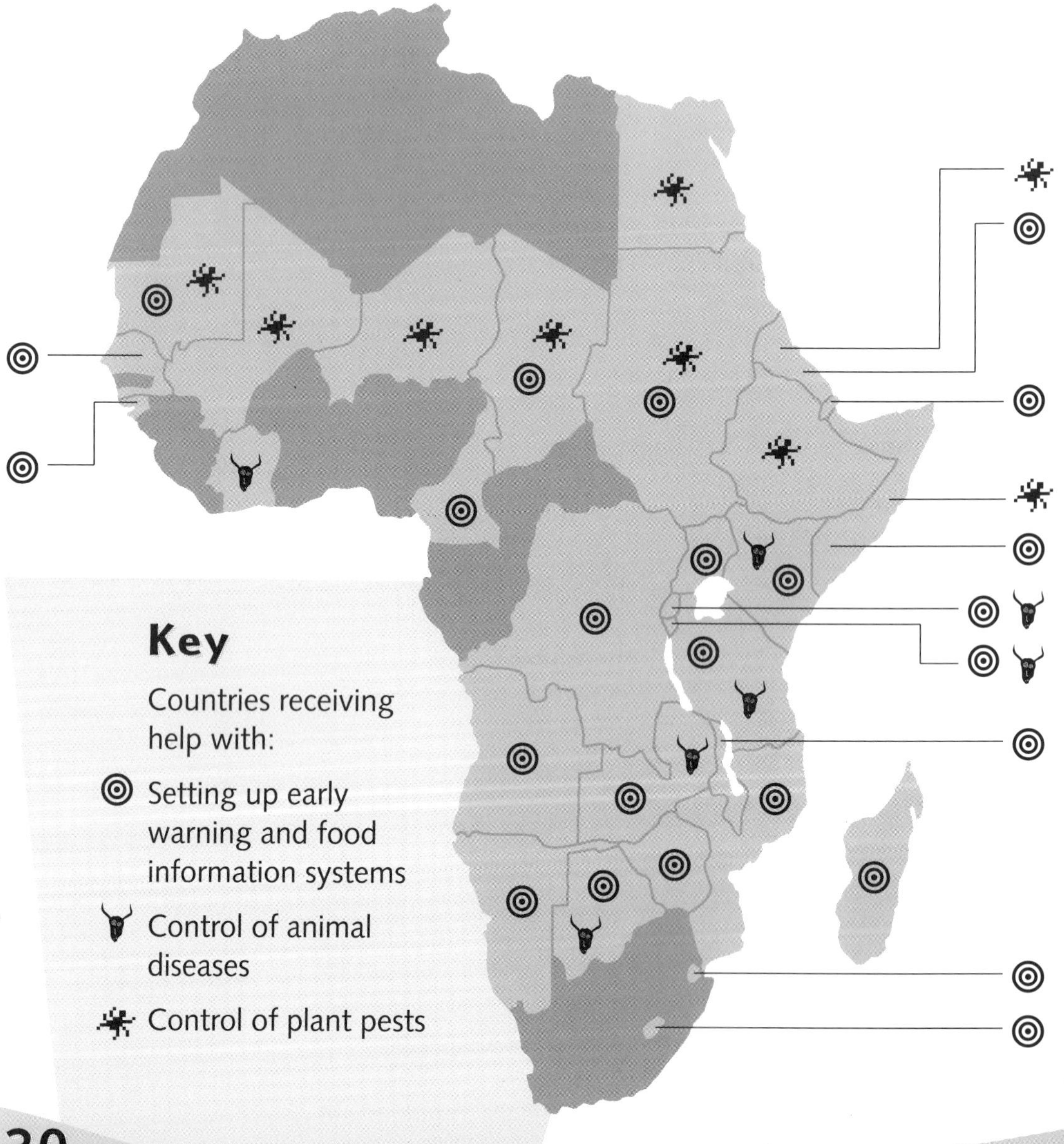

Key

Countries receiving help with:

◎ Setting up early warning and food information systems

🐃 Control of animal diseases

🕷 Control of plant pests

Glossary

agency a body of people working to help a government

carbon dioxide a gas which is heavier than air

conserve to protect, use wisely

crust the thin, solid surface of the earth

environment what is around us

erode to wear away by wind and water

evacuation taking people out of places of danger

famine large-scale hunger which leads to many deaths

fertile able to produce good crops

invasion marching or moving into a place

lightning rod a metal pole that carries lightning safely into the ground

molten hot and liquid

monitor to check what is happening in a situation

oasis a place in the desert where there is water

oxygen a gas in the air we breathe which is needed for life

plate a sheet of rock forming part of the earth's crust

plateau a high area of land

policy a plan of action

precaution an action taken for safety's sake

predict to decide what is likely to happen

regulations a set of rules

resistant able to fight

sandstorm a desert storm of wind with clouds of sand

silt fine fertile mud carried by rivers

surge to move forward in a rush

surplus more than is needed

swarm a huge number of insects

tides the movement in the earth's oceans

tremors small shaking movements

vaccination an injection of medicine

vegetation plants growing in an area

wetland a place which is normally covered by water or very wet

Index

animal diseases 27, 30
conservation 11, 31
crust of earth 18–19, 31
cyclones *see* storms
diseases 8
    animal 27, 30
drought 10–11
    map of 7
    preparing for 29
earthquakes 16–17
    and floods 8
    list of 24
    maps of 7, 22–3
    preparing for 29
famine 5, 10, 31
FAO (Food and Agricultural Organisation) 27, 30
farming
    and animal diseases 27, 30
    and drought 10, 11
    and floods 8, 9
    and pests 5, 7, 26
fertile soil 9, 31
fires 13
floods 5, 8–9
    map of 7
    preparing for 29
food *see* FAO; farming
forest fires 13
gas from volcanoes 19, 20–1
hurricanes *see* storms
insects, damage by 5, 7, 26
invasion 26, 31
landslide 5

lava 18–19
lightning 13, 31
locusts and grasshoppers 5, 7, 26
maps 7, 22–3, 30
molten rock 18, 31
monitoring 21, 22, 31
Nyos, Lake 20–1, 22, 24
oasis 6, 31
Paracutin, Mount 18, 22
plants
    as food *see* farming
    as pests 28, 30
sandstorm 6, 31
silt 9, 31
storms (cyclones and hurricanes) 5, 12, 13, 14–15
    lightning 13, 31
    preparing for 29
surge 8, 31
tides 8, 31
tsunamis 8
volcanic eruptions 18–25
    list of 24
    making your own 25
    maps of 7, 22–3
    Nyos, Lake 20–1, 22, 24
    preparing for 29
water
    hyacinth 28
    saving 11
    too little *see* drought
    too much *see* floods
waves, giant 8
wetland 9, 31
winds *see* cyclones